THE YEAR OF 2021

Covid-19: One year later

Nohad T. Harati

To my nephew, Philippe, who will reap the rewards of a job well done.

INTRODUCTION

The year that started with a lot of optimism soon was fogged by a series of uncertainties. As vaccine distribution began, the world was overwhelmed by more contagious virus variants. Economies had to be shut down again, although this time each country took individual circumstances into account when evaluating trade-offs.

For authorities at large, it became clear that economies had to be held for longer, requiring further fiscal spending, not to mention new initiatives. As Christine Lagarde, President of the European Central Bank (ECB) brilliantly put it, getting the pandemic behind not necessarily meant returning to previous economic arrangements.

As soon as the fog lifts, what is it that society in general will encounter? Topics include anything from the fear of higher inflation (and subsequent interest rate adjustments bursting asset price bubbles) to enlarged inequality gaps. All of which require governments and organized groups to discuss a new form of social contract, determining what future the next generation will live in.

This will inevitably lead to a redefinition of social goods, private ownership, use of natural resources, and the role of governments in addressing issues such as pension costs and universal basic income. All in a sustainable way as a "once in a lifetime" pandemic leaves little room for error.

The purpose of this book is to enlighten minds on the path that will lead the world to a new form of functioning, however clumsy the process might be, considering that covid-19 (and the new variants that may yet develop) will still be around for some time.

CONTENTS

1 – CHINA
2 – BITCOIN
3 – GAMESTOP
4 – SPACs
5 – UNIVERSAL BASIC INCOME
6 – TREASURY YIELDS
7 – NFT
8 – ARCHEGOS CAPITAL MANAGEMENT
9 – VIRTUAL CLIMATE SUMMIT
10 – GOVCOINS
11 – CAPEX
12 – GEOPOLITICS
13 – GREEN CRYPTOS
14 – CYBER ATTACKS
15 – DELTA
16 – STARTUP FRENZY
17 – STAGFLATION
18 – DEFI
19 – ENERGY CRISIS
20 – UNAFFORDABLE HOUSING
21 – THIRD WAVE
22 – GLOBAL VENTURE
23 – THE FUTURE

CHAPTER 1

CHINA

About 20 years ago, Jim O'Neill, an economist at Goldman Sachs, an investment bank, published a report highlighting the strength of the so-called BRICs (Brazil, Russia, India, and China).

According to calculations of that time, these countries would represent 20% of global GDP, given their high growth rates and, partially offsetting Europe's performance, as the continent was busy implementing the euro (currency).

Since then, the balance between the four countries has changed. If China and Brazil once had similar weights in emerging markets' main indices, today China participates with 40%. In other words, despite the BRICs (South Africa was only included in 2010) output of US$ 20 trillion, much of this performance is due to China.

The letter "C" comes first

In a period of no more than 40 years, China left the eighth position to become the second biggest economy in the world (the US being the first). Responsible for roughly 30% of global growth, it is the main business partner to 120 countries.

According to International Monetary Fund (IMF) estimates, China will be the largest economy of the planet as soon as 2030. With a numerous and rich population (income of US$ 10,000 per capita) it is by itself a gigantic consumer market.

If China was once famous for its cheap exports and heavy infrastructure spending, now the country works on the sustainable growth of its own demand. Located in a region where there are more individuals than the rest of the world combined, it is impossible to ignore its gravitational force.

Planning ahead

In 2020, China posted a 2.3% GDP growth, something unimaginable when considering how much the pandemic changed the world. Only economy to show positive figures, what differentiates its performance from the rest is its political regime. State capitalism, like any form of capitalism, is a growth inducer, even if the incentive is the government's strict five-year plan.

It is no wonder then that the country grew 36 times in the last 30 years, something that the US took 117 years to achieve. This applies even when the world economy falters. In these cases, it is not unusual for Chinese local authorities to receive a call from Beijing demanding the construction of more infrastructure, factories and buildings.

Although this generates excess capacity in the country, not to mention diminishing marginal benefits to the economy, this is how the Chinese political elite remains in power. After all, economic growth is good, and this applies outside China.

The Belt and Road Initiative is the offspring of this development model. Aimed at financing big infrastructure projects to a group of countries that can barely afford them, it not only ships abroad its enormous industrial capacity but also secures access to commodities, including agricultural ones.

Xi Jinping's generation

The new generation, identified as "jiulinghou", totals 188 million people (more than the population of England, Australia and Germany combined), although China has adopted a one child policy in the 1980s.

That's that best educated generation the country ever had: 9 million graduates start working every year, joined by the 80% of international students that return home once their study years are over. Highly qualified in STEM areas (Science, Technology, Engineering, and Mathematics), they bear the burden of a work routine that includes 12 hours per day, 6 days per week.

It is not by chance that China is the place where most billionaires are "created".

Technology

By far the best stock exchange performer, technology is one of the growth paths of the region. In the same way that the country invested heavily in physical infrastructure, it is praised for how much it invests in digital infrastructure.

Currently, there are more tech companies in the country than in the US and Europe combined. They cater to 800 million internet users, which is equivalent to the sum of the entire population of the US, Indonesia and Brazil.

China is the largest venture capital investor in the world since 2018. While Americans take an average of 7 years to produce a unicorn (startup worth more than US$ 1 billion), the Chinese achieve the same in 4 years, with approximately half of them acquiring this privileged status in just 2 years.

This effect is nowhere more visible than in the Star Market

(Chinese Nasdaq). Founded in 2019, it has launched more than 200 companies, with a pipeline containing twice as much potential IPO companies. With such fierce competition, major players pick and choose their bets on the largest of scales.

Super apps like WeChat are the result. It is nothing more than the bundling of all products developed by the start-ups that, in one way or another, received venture capital funding.

Sure bet

All in all, China can't be ignored. In the middle of a pandemic year, the country broke export records, which is something outstanding considering the enormous logistical difficulties faced by all of its 120 business partners.

Having guaranteed access to fundamental markets, it has evolved to the exponential growth only technology can offer. Counting on enough brains and digital infrastructure, it already has its own tech capital market, boosted by important companies that invest in just about everything.

Regardless of what is agreed on tariffs for Chinese goods or how the trade war evolves, the truth is that there is plenty of money to be made in terms of tech, including e-commerce models that blend shopping experience with social media, games, messaging, and live events.

This is definitely a trend that will stick, helping businesses operate under any circumstances.

CHAPTER 2

BITCOIN

The creation of bitcoin is unique, to say the least:
- Little is known about Satoshi Nakamoto, apparently responsible for its creation
- Everything started with 50 coins, called the "genesis block"
- The code includes the date of January 3rd, 2009 and the cover story of the Financial Times reporting the second bailout program for banks hit by the 2008 financial crisis

Bitcoin became trendy in 2013, when its price hit US$ 1,000. Since then, it has performed quite erratically. Having reached US$ 19,000 in December 2017, it lost 80% of its value the following year. In the beginning of 2021, it set new records, exceeding US$ 50,000.

This time, however, there is a logic behind those numbers.

Wall Street

If in the past cryptos were limited to libertarians opposing a currency controlled by governments or central banks, now Wall Street is starting to embrace it, for practical reasons.

The first one is due to its scarcity. Limited to 21 million units available, it works as a hedge against inflation, performing a similar role to gold in financial markets. The second reason is due to the fact that bitcoin requires no vaults for proper storage, only a digital wallet.

Both compensate for the obvious flaw, which is its high correlation to the stock market (both move in the same direction). Liquidity is also an issue when compared to other financial assets, as bitcoin tends to suffer wild price fluctuations.

In other words, in the same way that crypto volatility attracts hedge funds, it scares off other important participants such as pension funds, who fear enormous reputational risk when trading anything that is not yet regulated.

Diversification

Despite an entire ecosystem created around cryptocurrencies, crypto theft and exchange bankruptcies are the reasons why most asset managers prefer to steer clear. But, in a world where everything else is very expensive, reducing potential gains, many are considering bitcoin for diversification, albeit in a lower percentage of portfolios.

There is no denying that things are moving in that direction, especially after the crypto exchange Coinbase announced plans to go public. Once it can trade its shares just like any other company, it is just a matter of time for crypto assets to be launched, such as a crypto index funds (ETFs), for example.

Counting on the privileged conditions offered by a fully regulated market (credibility and liquidity), demand would then be generated by the millions of retail investors with a free brokerage account.

Investing spree

In a very low interest rate environment, people buy shares for the simple fact that any return is better than none.

After all, well-known tools such as fundamental analysis

are very reliable in predicting returns. This has been proved by economist Robert Shiller, 2013 Nobel Prize winner, in a study conducted in 1988 with a colleague.

It still applies to today's world. According to data gathered by Shiller, the longer the analysis period, the more precise it tends to be given that it smooths out the impact of unusual years, barely influencing the long-term.

However exciting that might be, there is one undeniable truth that many ignore: very low interest rates inflate asset prices. When stocks outperform, returns in the following years tend to be lower.

This pattern is also seen in other assets, such as real estate. For instance, when the value of real estate exceeds the expected return in rents, the result is a lower return rather than a higher rent.

Considering bitcoin itself, an "asset" that has no future cashflow to measure against, its valuation is nothing more than financial agents' perception of risk (greed versus fear).

"TINA"

In a nutshell, bitcoin might become more expensive simply because "There Is No Alternative".

Due to its limited supply, all it needs is a large enough demand. Whether the initial purchases come from Tesla or a hedge fund, retail investors soon enough jump in the bandwagon, expecting to make money more out of volatility than any fundamentals.

Professional investors will inevitably exploit whatever herd behavior there is, as they are all well aware of the low returns ahead.

Regulation wise, it is well-known that authorities refuse to see bitcoin as a currency since it does not have all of its three attributes: means of exchange, a unit of account and, more importantly, a store of value.

As central banks develop their versions of digital currencies (Central-Bank Digital Currency - CBDC), they tend to have concerns of their own, such as money laundering, the impact of negative interest rates in the economy (which harm commercial banks), and the distribution of government aid programs (something the pandemic has shown as extremely handy).

In the meantime, there is no intention to abolish bank notes or limit their circulation.

CHAPTER 3

GAMESTOP

As mentioned in my previous book "The Year of 2020 in 20 Chapters: How Covid-19 Reshaped the World and Financial Markets", at some point, retail investors were given access to the derivatives world, through options traded on online platforms.

The setting could not be more appropriate. Covid-19 provided the right turbulence for options to become fashionable. By August of last year, the number of daily traded calls was already bigger than the number of shares traded themselves (more than 3 times the average of the 3 previous years). Thus, it was just about a matter of time for social media to leave its impact on stock prices.

In the last week of January, a big group with a catchy name on Reddit ("WallStreetBets") caused havoc. As each group member posted gains on a once unloved video game retailer stock, more would pile in, seduced by the idea that anyone with a free brokerage account can beat professional hedge fund managers ("the establishment").

Day traders ("little fish") were fighting against the short-sellers ("sharks" of the hedge fund industry), following the same rationale of video games.

The logic behind this "battle" was that the company was undervalued as it had plans to move into e-commerce, becoming rather like a tech firm ("day traders' gamble").On the other hand, no matter how high prices would get, they were still limited to fundamentals ("short sellers' gamble").

The more day traders bought, the more prices were out of their expected range, squeezing short sellers. GameStop, which has a value of less than US$ 200 million in 2020 became a company worth US$ 24 billion in early 2021.

The case's biggest controversy was if the Securities and Exchange Commission (SEC) had to intervene, as price manipulation is extremely hard to prove among so many anonymous internet users following their own judgement as to what they should do with their money.

Soon enough, brokerage houses themselves started imposing restrictions, especially after similar movements were seen with other stocks, in circumstances that did not reflect the usual flow of business.

Forgotten after a few weeks, what this episode teaches is that the little guy can't beat the hedge fund manager, no matter the number of daily downloads of Robinhood's app. Stock markets remained unbothered, as GameStop barely had any effect on their overall performance.

CHAPTER 4

SPACs

In 2020, the US had 250 listed Special Purpose Acquisition Companies (SPACs), totaling US$ 83 billion. By the beginning of 2021, Europe and Asia were quickly adding their own.

The process is much faster, due to the fact that it avoids the traditional and costly IPO. A group of investors fund a shell (empty) company so that it can merge with another that wishes to go public. A SPAC usually undergoes the following steps:

1. A sponsor launches it
2. Investors pay for a certain number of shares (and warrants, in case they wish to buy more in following funding rounds).
3. The sponsor looks for companies suitable to merge
4. Shareholders vote before the deal is closed
5. Once merged, the sponsor receives shares of the new company, together with a board seat, in order to actively participate in management

As much as the procedure itself is quite simple, it exposes the changes the pandemic has brought to financial markets in general.

For many years, tech companies grumbled over investment banks' absolute control of public offerings, not to mention the hefty fees charged (between 5% and 7%). For no other reason, direct listings became popular: with the support of high-frequency dealers, founders and staff could sell their shares directly to others, cashing out on their holdings.

Quite flexible, SPACs have allowed for all sorts of arrangements, making it very hard for investors to study each of them individually. Notably, the best ones are run by traditional players such as private equity funds or former Fortune 500 executives. Even so, finding valuable companies became tricky with so many SPACs coming to life.

Poor results can be expected down the road, as celebrities help promote fanciful ideas. Looking back, most fall far from making stellar results. Considering SPACs that have been around since 2019, many have lost a third of their value one year after the merger.

That doesn't mean they are not appropriate to fund venture capital initiatives or companies that develop nascent technologies. As a matter of fact, they represent the only opportunity for retail investors to participate in the early stages of development, which usually bring in the biggest rewards.

CHAPTER 5

UNIVERSAL BASIC INCOME

In the absence of mass vaccination schedules early in the pandemic, governments rolled out poverty relief programs instead. As financing in the markets was still cheap, the discussion of a universal basic income came forward, especially for the fact that unemployment programs long needed an overhaul.

US figures covering a 20-year period showed that the number of unemployed people aged between 25 and 54 increased by 25%, barely 6 times the number of people under government assistance programs.

In today's world, when out of a job, most become gig workers, remaining outside whatever job scheme is available. That said, shouldn't different programs apply? Why not look at Denmark, a country that provides citizens with a new set of skills?

Emergency aid

Emergency programs benefited from the wonders of technology (internet and digital accounts) to rapidly distribute resources during lockdowns. One year later, many were left pondering if this experience could be adapted to other purposes.

As aid was delivered directly to households, there was an unexpected rise in entrepreneurship (particularly in the US), as incomes increased by 15.6% after government cheques were distributed.

Welfare versus income

Looking at the most common welfare state models, they usually include one or more of the following characteristics:

- Alleviate poverty
- Society bears part of the cost
- It is handed according to certain conditions

All due to the fact that capitalism has its own limits. For no other reason, Friedrich Hayek, an economist, proposed a universal basic income program to address unemployment resulting from technological change.

Inequality also plays a bigger role now, since the last decade increased the wealth gap between asset holders and the ever-increasing number of self-employed people. As fortunes concentrate at the top, policy makers ask themselves how to redistribute without wrecking government budgets.

That is not an easy question. In the Swiss referendum of 2016, when asked to vote for a universal basic income of US $ 2,500, 80% of the population rejected it, fearing higher taxes to fund the program.

Even so, economists follow this matter closely.

Social laboratory

In a period of 10 years, 16 basic income programs evaluated the impacts in rich and poor countries alike. Even when accounting for country disparities, results were promising: recipients not only did not quit their work, but also went further, developing new skills. As a result, they presented better physical and mental health.

However valuable for the future of public policy, no program was ever held on a national scale. Whatever model selected, each country has to be mindful of the costs. All programs require substantial funding, whether through the taxation of wealth, carbon emissions or even digital services.

The balance between letting people work as they see fit and the price of this privilege is yet to be found.

CHAPTER 6

TREASURY YIELDS

In the end of February, 10-year US Treasury bond yields jumped above 1.6%.

Although low by historical standards (around 3.5% a decade ago), this move said a lot about what was not known back then. As an indicator of confidence, was it increasing due to an expected recovery ahead or was it for fear of higher inflation?

Consumption has been postponed due to the pandemic and savings had never been higher, topped by government aid programs.

Given the circumstances, what was supposed to happen next? Many believed returning to "normal" would lead to an increase in US interest rates faster and in a more intense way than predicted by the Fed. For no other reason, Treasury auctions were disappointing, with financial institutions refusing to buy more bonds.

Even when they were willing to trade between themselves, transactions occurred with big discounts in prices, deteriorating financial conditions and directly affecting borrowers and investors alike.

More often than not, central banks end up intervening when they see excesses. The secret is not to create a bigger problem than the one being addressed.

Helicopter money

Unlike the 2008 crisis, no one was being shy this time. Instead of just one, governments were using simultaneously many helicopters to distribute money.

One year after the beginning of the pandemic, Americans had accumulated roughly US$ 1.6 trillion. This big pile of money eventually had to go somewhere, not least for consumption, as retail indicators early in the year showed.

When the US is that vibrant, international trade thrives, boosting the world economy. The question was how consistent spending would be, as average citizens could expect tax increases down the road to help pay for all the government largesse.

Economists clumsily tried to answer. Estimates went from recovering pre-pandemic levels to a 6.2% GDP growth. Disparity in numbers was mainly due to the fact that people have different perceptions about income and wealth, influencing their decisions when it comes to money.

According to a few studies, people tend to spend more their income (boosted by government cheques) than their wealth (increase in value of a portfolio of stocks). Nonetheless, the risk that Americans wound go on a binge existed, impacting monetary policy.

Central guardians

After the inflationary period that marked the 60s and 70s, central banks were given the job of maintaining price stability. By delegating them this function, it was believed monetary policy could be isolated from reckless politicians seeking reelection.

This view proved to be adequate, as central banks took an important role in the economic recovery after the 2008 crisis. Seen as better prepared, they acted more decisively. However, roughly a decade later, their main instruments (interest rate setting and bond purchasing programs) were touching their limits, as asset prices reached all-time highs in the beginning of 2020.

With the arrival of the pandemic, together with inequality issues, fiscal policy was coordinated with the active participation of central banks, in order to keep financial markets' risks in check. Inflating new asset bubbles were a concern, reason why the extra effort had to be temporary.

Although the Fed has a primary purpose of assuring price stability and low unemployment, it is well aware of the impacts of its monetary policy in other parts of the world (currency devaluations and restrictive corporate credit, to name a few).

CHAPTER 7

NFT

NFT, or "non-fungible token", is nothing more than a blockchain-based code that authenticates virtual art pieces such as video, photo, music or any other group of digital data. As they are mercilessly copied everywhere, what NFTs try to do is provide the same rigor as the one applied to the traditional art market.

In the beginning of 2021, NFTs as a group represented US $ 300 million, perfectly reflecting the speculative nature of markets when in low interest rate environments. As Alan Greenspan, former chairman of the Fed used to say, that's "irrational exuberance".

Exclusivity
The art world always rotated around the concept of exclusivity, having a dynamic of its own.

Art becomes fashionable when investment opportunities elsewhere vanish. This is due to the fact that collectibles lack liquidity. The internet, however, fostered an increase in the number of transactions, as authenticity certificates and auction prices can now be checked online. As a result, art became eligible as collateral (guarantee) for loans.

If this market took off because of low interest rates, social media gave it an extra boost. Gone are the days when economists focused on studying behavioral finance, considering how individual decisions are made once exposed to the effects of virtual networks.

Changes in risk perception and FOMO become predominant, altering the ultimate purpose of directing savings to the best investment opportunities.

Limitations

The market for NFTs is far from perfect. The mining activity behind it to validate blockchain transactions is energy intensive. For no other reason, it is carried out in the most polluting places in the world.

The second problem is that NFTs can be detached from their original work, allowing for modifications even after they are sold. In the absence of a secondary registration system, chances are agents will hardly do any business as they lack trust in this market.

It is a fact that many virtual initiatives have failed in the past, the most memorable example being initial coin offerings (ICOs).

Used to finance innovation, they were heavily promoted without the burdens of financial regulation or the distribution costs charged by investment banks. Promising juicy returns, they became very popular, even though were based on a very fragile model.

Back then, enormous amounts were being placed with nothing more than a blockchain platform, created for a specific purpose, and a 20-page white paper. ICOs were able to raise US$ 13 billion in just 5 months before they were forgotten.

In the venture capital world, only 1 out of 10 ideas are successful in the way people know it. Serial failures happen before a suitable standard is set.

Just like art in the real world, NFTs will make no one rich unless it can count on a reliable market.

CHAPTER 8

ARCHEGOS CAPITAL MANAGEMENT

As explained in my book "Family Offices in Brazil: An overview of financial products, family wealth and future trends", the origins of a family office can vary, including the following groups:

- A family that decides to float its company
- A successful internet entrepreneur that wishes to fund new businesses
- A hedge fund manager that goes solo

Although they all aim to professionally manage financial assets, they work differently. In the case of the family, funds are invested in order to perpetuate wealth for the next generations. That said, it is the most traditional model of them all.

The digital entrepreneur, on the other hand, directs investments to businesses found in the internet world, promoting innovation. Venture Capital (VC) and seed capital are the main destinations, being losses part of the game.

Lastly, there are those that learned the path to riches by investing other people's money. That's the hedge fund elite. For this group, bullish or bearish markets really don't matter, as long as profits can be made by exploiting their inefficiencies ("absolute returns").

Archegos Capital Management

Many have heard of George Soros, but few know Bill Hwang, a former hedge fund manager responsible for a US$ 20 billion forced stock sale that dragged along major players like

Credit Suisse (Europe) and Nomura (Japan).

Hwang is a tiger cub from Tiger Management, legendary firm belonging to Julian Robertson. Specialized in Asian markets, Hwang decided to apply his knowledge of decades (since the 90's) in his own family office, named Archegos Capital Management.

Archegos' strategy is well known. It is nothing more than the purchase of certain shares and the sale of others, so a gain is made regardless of market sentiment. Given its sheer size, Hwang was able to operate through OTC markets, without the obligation to disclose Archegos positions.

Despite being effective in most cases, it's not quite suited for "black swan" events, such as a pandemic.

Leverage

If there is something experienced hedge fund managers have access to is their contact list. When setting their own shops, they obtain better financing conditions and terms, although other financial intermediaries are not always aware of all the risks they are exposed to.

In Archegos' case, brokers did more than just execute orders. They also provided loans and assets. With a leveraged portfolio, it only took ViacomCBS (a media company) to perform badly to leave a margin call unfulfilled, leading to the liquidation of the fund's global positions.

Goldman Sachs and Morgan Stanley were faster to act, leaving Credit Suisse and Nomura with billion-dollar losses, something that ended up reflecting on their own share prices (Nomura's shares fell 16% in a single day).

Volcker Rule

A regular investor's natural reaction would be to ask why

first-class financial institutions get involved in such risky transactions. The truth is that life for them became much more difficult after the Volcker Rule. A consequence of the 2008 crash, banks no longer could engage in proprietary trading (trades on their own accounts).

In order to make money, they set up arrangements similar to Archegos, in exchange of service fees and commissions. With the pandemic, this gained gargantuan proportions, as banks shifted away from credit, more directly related to the real economy, to focus on the more profitable financial markets.

Long-Term Capital Management

Hwang's family office is not an isolated case.

Rescued by a plan coordinated by the Federal Reserve (Fed) in 1998, Long-Term Capital Management (LTCM) also operated highly leveraged, mainly due to the talent pool behind it: a star trader (John Meriwether) and two Nobel Prize economists (Robert Merton and Myron Scholes) responsible for developing the option pricing model with Fischer Black ("Black and Scholes" model).

LTCM's main strategy was to search for asset pairs that differed between them. Once a pair was chosen, the most expensive asset was sold while the cheapest was purchased. As the gap narrowed, the fund made profits in both ends. The difference represented pennies most of the time but, due to leverage, the fund was able to exploit no less than 38,000 asset pairs.

Numbers would have been bigger were it not for Russia, who defaulted on its debt in 1998. With the crash, came the bailout. The fund had so many large positions that undoing them would increase the price difference between the asset pairs, potentially bankrupting LTCM.

No matter how skilled or rich, these big investors are exposed to the same unforeseen global risks, as the pandemic has shown.

CHAPTER 9

VIRTUAL CLIMATE SUMMIT

One of the big events of the year, its intention was to bring back America's leading role in global affairs. Although it was not clear how countries would meet increasingly ambitious reduction targets, the purpose of the event was to set a common ground for a post-pandemic recovery.

On the agenda, the so-called NDCs, scheduled greenhouse emission reductions that countries present to the United Nations. Established in 2013, they were supposed to adapt to each country's priorities, eliminating the problems generated by the Kyoto Protocol, which imposed targets on developed countries, but left China, a big polluter, out.

With the Paris Agreement, more countries joined, committing themselves to elaborate on doable action plans at the COP26 (United Nations conference). As a trade-off, a new form pf economic growth, less damaging to the environment and better suited to address inequality.

Execution

How to execute these action plans, however, is another matter. Zeroing carbon emissions by 2050 means recreating the world we live in. According to the International Energy Agency (IEA), this is yet to happen as it depends on technologies that do not exist today.

Many rich countries use the proceeds of oil sales to subsidize research and development. Norway is a notable example, as it has advanced in manipulating carbon in several ways, capturing it, transporting it, and storing it.

The same cannot be said about emerging markets, partly due to NDCs' design, which had to be adapted in order to please more reluctant nations. For this group, fighting climate change also involves other sensitive issues such as intellectual property and industrial policy.

As these areas are barely shared worldwide, a gap between rich and emerging countries is expected, both in terms of economic and technological development, eliminating all the benefits of globalization.

Financing

In order to finance green energy innovation, SPACs (explained in chapter 4).

The question is where to invest going forward. This difficulty is justified by the lack of information in unlisted companies, many of which are barely more than an idea in search of money. As a result, many perform poorly, as they use overly optimistic estimates.

Fortunately, markets adjust for excesses, albeit not benefitting everyone. Emerging countries, although different from what they were in the 80's, still carry the stigma of past defaults. This means every time the US raises interest rates, they face prohibitive financing costs, in addition to devalued financial assets (as seen in 2013's "taper tantrum").

Economies try to defend themselves, reducing their dependence on foreign money or technology. The result is a series of local arrangements, poorly developed in terms of what they can offer to promote corporate research and innovation programs.

Once the "virtual" aspect of the summit is gone, now it is

time to understand how countries will navigate in this new geopolitical landscape. This is because climate change is far from just caring about plants and animals.

Rich countries have a major head start, which gives them plenty of room to experiment. The same cannot be said about other big economies that lack both the technology and the means to keep up.

CHAPTER 10

GOVCOINS

When it comes to money, it inevitably has to fulfill 3 requirements:
1. Means of exchange: in order to pay for goods and services
2. Unit of account: a numeric representation of a transaction
3. Store of value: instrument for wealth formation

At the height of the 2008 financial crisis, it was believed that bitcoin could replace national currencies, given that governments were embracing inflationary risks as they tried to address the consequences of excessive leverage.

These risks did not materialize and the world has changed since then. Advances provided by the internet kept inflation at persistently low levels. Without the need to raise interest rates, asset prices went nowhere but up, leaving few opportunities to explore.

As bitcoin increasingly becomes an "asset", due to its technology and scarcity, its volatility prevents it from turning into a store of value. For no other reason, monetary authorities from all over the world have embarked on their own initiatives, launching govcoins (government digital currencies).

e-currencies

No financial system survives without some form of control, no matter how innovative.

Given the resources available today, this system could even be simpler, providing everyone a chance to use it for daily activities without the hassle of a banking network. Hence, the purpose of e-currencies.

Everything started a few years ago, when China was on its way to developing its own digital currency. Since then, 50 countries have joined, including tiny jurisdictions like Bahamas. But, unlike the traditional financial system, where the US dollar has a major role, govcoins offer a more leveled playing field.

This e-race has its logic. Central banks conduct monetary policy. By allowing tech companies to development their own money systems, how capable are they of stabilizing a country's economic conditions once facing adversity?

Additionally, the implementation of government digital currencies eliminates a series of costs from the financial system, either because that's the only thing available or because everyone depends on it. In the urgency to fix several constrains, a mechanism where the central bank itself offers a digital account, with all the convenience one can think of.

No freedom

The other side of e-currencies, however, concerns financial freedom. In the pilot project conducted in China to stimulate the economy, emergency aid beneficiaries had a deadline to spend the money, in a time when they would rather save.

For governments, other benefits would include facilitation in the collection of due taxes or the retrieval of illegal money. In extreme cases, capital flights could be stopped, something emerging economies have witnessed far too often.

Technically known as Central Bank Digital Currencies (CBDC), it's a fact govcoins are here to stay, regardless of what internet giants are doing. This topic obviously involves other issues, such as cybersecurity, for example.

All in all, countries lack alternatives. Worse than having their sovereignty threatened by companies bigger than many national GDPs, it is knowing that a currency can be replaced by another that is yet to be created.

For society at large, e-currencies will reshape habits and everyday life. What to buy, when and in what currency will be decisions that may or may not be defined by someone as distant as a central banker.

CHAPTER 11

CAPEX

Unlike day trading, investing in a publicly traded company is betting on its fundamentals: markets, cash flow, debt levels, among other things.

As the pandemic showed, companies that were better prepared survived and, unlike previous crises, had access to credit lines. As a result, many decided to merge, making them increasingly relevant.

Throughout the year, a series of investment projects were implemented, setting a trend for the future. Considering 2022 alone, companies that are part of the S&P 500 will most likely be investing 10% more in new facilities and technologies, as shown in quarterly results.

That's quite a change. Looking over the last decades, capex investment levels in the US have remained constant in relation to GDP, as companies started to favor share buyback programs and greater dividend distribution.

As much as that might please shareholders, the results observed over time were low growth and low productivity.

Capex

Reopening economies were not the only reason for spending. New investments were due to the adaptations people have made in their lives. A greater share of online purchases means transaction back-up systems need upgrading.

Large technology companies invested 30% more when

compared to 2019. This could be seen in machine and equipment investment as well. According to the most optimistic estimates, by 2022, the world will have invested 121% more than before the pandemic.

The belief of a fast economic recovery was the main driving force. All because people would continue to do more things from home, making even the most traditional sectors digitize their operations in order not to lose market share.

It is too early to say whether this process is just a result of unique circumstances. More cyclical sectors, such as commodities, remained the same, with supply only increasing when prices are higher. In the absence of new competitors, few had the appetite to invest.

The truth is that every investor should look where the money is going. Is it being directed to better serve the customer or is it just being recycled through buyback or dividend programs?

That's a fundamental question. When companies do not invest, they limit their opportunities. As observed in the US stock market, lack of investment goes hand in hand with low productivity.

The pandemic may be changing this. With such low interest rates, corporations are making projects viable in a way that hasn't been seen for a long time. Promising prospects are everywhere, ranging from tech companies that need to provide a robust infrastructure to those that are contemplating new ways of doing business.

CHAPTER 12

GEOPOLITICS

International investments. Who has never been fascinated by this topic?

In practical terms, this means having plenty of options. Bonds, Exchange Traded Funds (ETFs) and other financial products, ranging from developed economies to the so-called "frontier markets", a category that includes African nations or countries that have never been on investors' maps before.

The past

An undeniable truth is that everything changes, especially when it comes to the business environment. This makes the management of international assets a real challenge.

If 20 years ago everyone was betting on Europe, due to the introduction of the euro, today the continent has lost much of its beat. Political interference and the debt crisis that nearly dragged Greece postponed European integration plans.

Although counting with a monetary authority (ECB), countries still manage their national budgets independently, which means there is no tool to transfer funds to regions facing temporary difficulties. Inevitably, a series of meetings are held and a new fund is created.

Slow to keep up with the rest of the world, the old continent lacks a company as big as Apple. Numbers are revealing of how much it has lagged behind: the company founded by

Steve Jobs is worth more than the 30 companies that make up the German stock index (DAX). When compared to the French stock index (CAC), it is worth more than its 40 listed companies.

In addition to the difficulties of integrating different nations, other elements affected Europe particularly hard:
- Greater dependence on bank credit when compared to the US, which has the world's largest stock market
- Cultural and legal barriers, making it impossible for any business to reach the same scale of American and Chinese firms

The future

Looking at the next 20 years, it is clear that heavily indebted governments need new revenue sources. For no other reason, the global efforts to close the tax loopholes used by technology companies, based on two opposing principles:
1. Taxing where companies conduct their businesses, as the Europeans suggested
2. Imposing a minimum percentage (around 15%), as defended by the Americans

Estimated annual tax revenues would be anywhere between US$50 billion and US$80 billion.

Truth be told, little is known about the next 20 years. Globalization started reversing before the pandemic. As a result, defensive countries trying to impose new regulations and taxes for businesses that have revolutionized the world.

For those who would rather ignore governments and geopolitics, investing everything in bitcoin is definitely not an option.

CHAPTER 13

GREEN CRYPTOS

Currently, two forces drive the renewable energy industry: clean sources (wind and solar) and electric vehicles (EV). Although prices are much lower today, there is an enormous difference between government programs aimed at rebuilding economies and effective GDP results.

In order to achieve a 70% reduction in greenhouse emission targets, it would be necessary to invest 4 times more in renewable sources. For transportation, this means that 60% of vehicles would have to be EV (this percentage is only 5% today).

Roughly speaking, more than US$4 trillion would be needed for the world to provide metals to the green economy (a proportion 7 times higher than today's, according to the International Energy Agency).

That said, it is not just a matter of "retiring" a bunch of oil and gas wells. The challenge is how to serve a market with individual characteristics.

Inputs

Starting with inputs. Copper, a fundamental metal for the electricity sector, is already 70% more expensive. Additionally, renewables, highly dependent on batteries, require access to the geographically concentrated cobalt, lithium and nickel mines.

As an example, 70% of the demand for cobalt is supplied by the Democratic Republic of Congo, a country that exploits mines with barely any technology. Similar cases can be found in other parts of the world, many of which unstable enough to fuel geopolitical tensions.

Location

Renewable power plants are better suited where nature is more benign in terms of wind regime and solar radiation. Although wind turbines and solar panels are much more efficient today, large areas are still essential for them to be installed.

Government bureaucracy is the main problem in this case, affecting the entire industry that supplies the green economy.

Financing

Many metal reserves are located in extremely poor regions, which reduces the possibility of enough funding for projects that can increase supply.

Despite a plants' relatively low maintenance cost (there is no cost for using sunlight or the wind), initial investments are quite representative, generating a fertile ground for cryptoassets.

Cryptoassets

Despite all the debate over cryptocurrencies, the major regulatory boost will probably come from cryptoassets. Also known as tokens, they are nothing more than the digital representation of an asset or a credit that, in turn, can be exchanged for a service (charging an EV or purchasing clean energy, for instance).

As the infrastructure of digital assets is still being built, it is certain that trends such as decentralized finance (DeFi), explained in chapter 18, will spread to complementary areas of finance (credit and insurance), as long as they meet minimum requirements.

The green economy, driven by renewables and EVs, is the "new internet". However, in order to achieve the same results as the technology giants, there must be a fine tuning between public policies and promising businesses.

Dependent on natural resources and long-lasting batteries, clean energy demands a format that differs from globalization, making it impossible to use the structure of global chains that have supported the world economy until now.

Cooperation between governments, a reduction in bureaucracy and well-designed financial mechanisms are the three elements that will lead humanity to a sustainable growth.

CHAPTER 14

CYBER ATTACKS

In a corporate survey, publicly traded companies of 85 different nationalities mentioned "cyber threat" more often in the past 8 years.

Truth be said, businesses are still trying to address this type of risk correctly. Understanding it better and informing financial markets would greatly help in this regard, although many refuse to take the lead, fearing a market value re-pricing.

Ransomware

Speculation around digital currencies has only increased the number of those seeking to profit from the illegal access to data, inflating ransom values (a total of US$ 350 million in 2020 alone) and the importance of selected targets.

It is a fact that cryptocurrencies, despite not having all the attributes of a currency, have become the favored means of payment for this type of criminal activity. Operational 24 hours a day, 7 days a week, it is a market that is always open, regardless of where the hacker is.

Free from any control by the financial system, amounts can be transferred anonymously anywhere in the world. This means that, depending on the jurisdiction (country), they are easily converted into dollars, euros or any other currency accepted worldwide.

That said, curbing ransom payments depends on banning

this market altogether or regulating it. The first alternative is the least likely of them. First, because it hurts investors who suddenly cannot cash out their crypto positions. Second, because it favors a bigger use of cash.

Crypto exchanges

As the main trading venue for cryptocurrencies, these exchanges suffer little regulation when compared to banks, responsible for whatever is done by their account holders.

For anyone who has had the experience of sending funds to other parts of the world, it is impossible not to encounter the zeal of financial institutions when requesting documents and explanations.

This does not occur in crypto exchanges, where the process of registering new clients is quite simple, not to mention flawed. Additionally, in the transactions they carry out, although the blockchain tracks the cryptocurrency, it does not show the sender behind it, bringing extra concerns to the regulated agents they conduct business with.

Banks

One of the sectors that invest the most in security, banks are obvious targets. After all, today everything is done online and even when a clerk is required, the risk is not always mitigated. A breach is always opened from the inside, through a seemingly harmless downloaded program.

In one of the most spectacular heists in history, hackers managed to transfer via SWIFT no less than US$ 81 million that the Bangladeshi Central Bank held with the New York Fed. In another robbery, this time in India, programmers changed the codes of ATM machines, resulting in 15,000 cash withdrawals in just 2 hours, totaling roughly US$ 13.5

million.

Hacking is a comprehensive job as it does not always involve cash. It can also be aimed at collecting data on asset transactions, favoring insider trading. That said, banks feel compelled to update whatever technology they use. With more internet-connected devices and employees working from home, vulnerability has never been greater.

The fact that many hacker groups are supported by countries banned from the international financial system grants them the best brains and technological resources. All in order to circumvent sanctions.

Bitcoin and other cryptocurrencies' status, therefore, will depend largely on the solution to the following dilemma: repress it to fight criminal activity, cutting off its main financing, or regulate it and let speculation run wild, crippling a growing number of small investors.

CHAPTER 15

DELTA

As far as economic recoveries are concerned, new contagion waves are always dangerous.

The new coronavirus, identified as Delta, spread two to three times faster than its first version. Despite the fast pace of vaccination, many regions lagged behind, and no vaccine was 100% effective.

Regarding supply restrictions, the world also suffered from the lack of electronic components and the disruption of important logistical routes. To compensate, the service sector, still quite shy, but which tended to react as people felt safe to leave home.

However, two unknown factors gained prominence going forward. One was the end of aid programs. The other was the expiration of financial relief measures adopted during the pandemic, such as the ban on evictions applied to defaulting tenants and the postponement of interest payments on loans.

Scarring

Among the various decisions taken by public and private entities to avoid permanent damages to the economy ("scarring"), the distribution of aid in cash to households and the job maintenance programs, in addition to loans on more favorable terms.

As they expired, many doubts emerged:

    1. Would the end of financial help derail consump-

tion?
2. Would the termination of employment programs leave many out of work?
3. Would the return of financial obligations cause the bankruptcy of companies and individuals?

The last was the hardest to predict as unpaid rents, taxes and loan installments went through a disorderly renegotiation process that needed fixing.

Indicators

In order to find answers, financial agents looked elsewhere:

1. Asset prices

Highly benefited since the start of the pandemic, asset prices shifted as expectations changed.

The July 19th scare, which disrupted the pricing of treasury bonds, S&P 500 shares and energy commodities, showed that there was not much belief in the reflation trade, a strategy where investors position themselves anticipating a recovery.

2. Mobility Data

Today, it is possible to monitor the activity in offices and stores. However, since official statistics are published with a certain delay, mobility data cannot be considered alone.

3. Real estate market

A quite heated market, transactions were carried out without potential buyers asking for any appraisal or visit to the properties themselves.

Reality

Important sector bodies, on the other hand, showed a different picture: 25% of tenants and 10% of mortgage holders did not know if they could keep their payments on time. Almost 3 million families had already stopped paying their rents while around 2 million homes were in default on their mortgages.

As it became clear, coronavirus mutations created the backdrop for a series of unsolved problems.

This meant that the real damage was yet to be evaluated as individuals and companies were called back to honor their financial commitments. As a result, a larger percentage could be out of income, jobs, or even housing.

Considering financial markets, this is the reality agents were picking up: a scenario with a lot of noise and frantic stock trading, but with barely any concrete results.

CHAPTER 16

STARTUP FRENZY

Starting with Robinhood's IPO on Nasdaq on July 29th.

Different from the regular practice, where investment banks fill out orders according to the financial capacity of institutional investors (funds, insurance companies, and family offices), it was decided that everyone should get a chance.

To participate, all it took was a 40-minute presentation aired on a weekend and an order to buy one share. Among the main attractions, a fintech valued at US$ 32 billion and that grew exponentially in the beginning of the pandemic, as people found themselves at home, receiving government help.

Expectations could not be higher but, on the day of its debut, the share price dropped 8.4%.

Order flow

Robinhood's business model of free stock trading only works as long as it is paid by high-frequency market makers.

Responsible for much of the order flow placed by retail investors to bet on GameStop (explained in chapter 3), the brokerage house was forced to suspend trading once unable to maintain activities in the 2-day settlement period necessary for shares to change hands.

Outraged, many investors turned to riskier alternatives such as derivatives and cryptocurrencies, precisely those for which Robinhood received the highest margins. All in favor of investing, as one of its founders strongly defended. As Robinhood continued opening new accounts, regulators stepped in.

Regulation

Regulation is one of the risks investors are generally unaware of.

China made headlines after it banned the IPO of one of Jack Ma's companies, imposed antitrust laws on local internet giants (Alibaba and Tencent), and impaired Didi's business shortly after its listing in the US.

Many believe Chinese authorities went overboard when they targeted a whole sector: new online learning startups were prohibited to go public, have foreign investors, or make any profits after regulations came into effect.

As a result, listed techs lost more than 60% of their market value, dragging along other companies on the Nasdaq and highlighting the regulatory risks all innovative businesses are exposed.

Unicorn

Perhaps the most extreme case is Nigeria. A place that has had payment fintechs for some time, the country finally gained its first unicorn (Interswitch, a payment processor).

Conditions there are hardly ideal: 95% of financial transactions are paid in cash, energy and telecom infrastructure is precarious, and 40% of the population earns less than US$ 1.90/day.

Government agencies are poorly equipped to regulate the sector. When in doubt, they veto other business models such as online loans and foreign stock trading platforms.

The same can be said about its central bank.

Hence, it is clear that high valuations are based solely on the size of the Nigerian population (almost 200 million) and the possible expansion across the African continent. As it is the case with China, it only takes a handful of troubled companies for an entire ecosystem to blow up.

Asset bubble

Low interest rates foster speculative bets, no matter how unreal startups can be. Given the number of stimuli to fight the economic consequences of the pandemic, it is feared that the side effects are yet to come.

The distinction between "Main Street" (the real economy) and "Wall Street" (the financial market) always comes to mind, sparking the debate over the role central banks should play, whether in relation to climate change or inequality.

One mission

At the height of globalization, it was common for central bankers to attribute inequality to factors beyond their control, such as the migration of entire production chains to places where costs were lower, leaving many out of work.

Monetary authorities claimed that they had a single mission (controlling inflation) and a single instrument (interest rates). Additionally, they recognized the limits of their economic models, which are nothing more than a simplification of reality.

As a result, they prefer to leave things as they are because they believe that, when considering other goals, they may achieve nothing, given the disruptive forces at work in the economy. As every central banker explains, running the economy is like shooting a moving target, something that requires much more skill and focus.

A more flexible approach is a better strategy than simply shooting everywhere. An inflation average rather than an inflation target, with all the implications that might have in financial markets.

CHAPTER 17

STAGFLATION

Stagflation is a combination of low growth, high inflation and high unemployment rates.

Although population in developed countries were already vaccinated, places where important supply chains were located faced continuous lockdowns, causing new price increases due to supply shocks.

The 70's

Contradicting the Phillips' curve, where inflation and unemployment have an inverse relationship, stagflation is new to those who were not yet born in the 70s. This was the time when the US faced high oil prices after OPEC's boycott. As a result, the US economy shrank while inflation took off.

Back then, given the geopolitical background, a greater stimulus to the economy would only cause more inflation, generating a vicious cycle that would do little to reduce unemployment. Hence, structural problems that unbalanced the economy needed to be addressed.

For no other reason, the implementation of extremely high interest rates, such as those adopted by Paul Volcker, chairman of the Fed, to bring the country back to a sustainable growth path.

Reversal

It is well known that government stimuli only work when used temporarily. With many of them being reversed or even subsidized through tax increases, the next obvious step is a raise in interest rates. For no other reason, emerging markets started their own monetary policy tightening.

Main economies, on their part, have some leeway due to asset purchase programs, which give them time to adjust before effectively recalibrating their interest rates, albeit far from the 70's levels. This is especially true for the Fed, concerned about the level of employment.

Inflation hedge

A global economy that barely grows but faces higher prices forces a portfolio rethink.

Under an inflationary scenario, bonds and stocks lose value, as their future cashflows are discounted at a higher rate. Assets such as real estate, farmland and infrastructure become more common, as contracts include inflation hedge clauses.

The challenge is imagining the impacts of climate change in projects that should provide income for decades. Are they pollutant enough to struggle under stricter rules? Will they be banned when seeking financing or insurance?

Business hedge

Another alternative is to invest in listed private equity companies that hold a stake in several businesses. This arrangement is an upgrade of the former private equity model.

Investors receive a share of the management fee, which tends to grow as assets under management become bigger. Additionally, they can cash part of their positions at any time, fostering a secondary market.

Lastly, it is flexible enough to issue more stocks as new deals emerge.

As the world economy reshapes itself, it is naïve to think a portfolio based on artificial intelligence (AI) will make anyone rich. After all, the generation behind the coding has not lived long enough to understand these new circumstances.

CHAPTER 18

DEFI

Decentralized finance (DeFi) is the latest promise in the field of finance, capable of addressing some of the limitations of the traditional financial system.

It is nothing more than a virtual infrastructure supported by blockchain technology (Ethereum), through which financial services are offered. It is a system that has evolved from two other equally important trends: the advance of fintechs and the issuance of digital government currencies (govcoins, as explained in chapter 10).

If traditionally money changes hands through an expensive and complex infrastructure, with prudential rules and its own legal framework, on the Ethereum platform this occurs through lines of coding that automatically perform a series of actions when certain conditions are met ("smart contracts").

Virtual investors have their own digital IDs, something similar to a social security number, and can store their digital assets through two ways: private keys (minding not to lose them) or an exchange (acting as a custodian).

This is where fraud and theft are most common. For no other reason, the growing adoption of smart contracts by the so-called decentralized exchanges.

Paradigm

In a DeFi environment, operations are not coordinated by a bank or a stock exchange, but rather by a decentralized autonomous organization (DAO).

To understand how that works, imagine a computer that runs a program. The computer, being a basic tool, allows for the development of anything, including digital assets.

Upgrades

Some virtual solutions stand out for addressing real life problems.

In order to fight currency volatility, stablecoins, digital currencies pegged to the US dollar or the euro. Far from flawless, their latest versions attach a basket of assets to a smart contract, making them automatically stabilize.

Arbitrage is another promising area. When a loan is taken to explore momentary opportunities, the borrower, when depositing a guarantee, receives and pays back the loan, together with a fee, within the same transaction blockchain, limiting the chances of default.

Limitations

One of DeFi's limitations is the blockchain technology itself. It is not yet scalable as each transaction group, or block, requires a certain amount of time to be added.

The other is its relationship with more traditional transactions. How this integration with the real world takes place is precisely what will define the finances of the future. A hybrid model could represent a first step, as DeFi gains some practical uses.

The truth is that there is no perfect system. For a new standard to emerge, the current one just needs to be exhausted.

CHAPTER 19

ENERGY CRISIS

Replacing a vital energy source is not an easy task, even when considering developed countries. As history itself shows, this process is quite slow, requiring major changes in infrastructure and in the functioning of the economy.

The result is not always what is expected. Although the new source steals part of the market share of the predominant energy source, its demand is barely impacted, as the market as a whole becomes bigger.

Drawing a parallel with current times, it is estimated that the cost of building new solar farms will be lower than the cost of maintaining thermal plants as early as 2030. This means that outdated fossil fuel plants will still be around for some time, given the cost of building new ones.

Gas Prices

Considering Europe's case, the Middle East cannot be blamed for soaring prices. Investments made by both Egypt and Israel in parts of the Mediterranean Sea provide natural gas, given the availability of liquefied natural gas (LNG) terminals.

A harsher winter in Europe and a hotter summer in Asia, due to climate change, increased energy consumption, at the same time that global production resumed. Unlike oil, gas has a relatively stable market, as it is also used for heating.

Demand

The green transition seemed well addressed a few years ago, thanks to investments in LNG terminals in the US, which benefited from shale technology, and the increasingly diversified project portfolio of European oil companies.

However, that has changed. Asia now imports roughly 75% of all LNG produced in the world. China specifically, having jump-started industrial production first, was not able to meet its 16% growth in energy consumption in the first half of 2021, even though 60% of the Chinese energy matrix is made up of coal.

With Asia in full swing, little was left for the rest of the world.

Supply

In the occurrence of energy supply shocks, it is common to turn to more polluting sources. This would not be so much of a trouble if it did not take place in Europe, supplied by gas super powers such as Russia and Norway, and where energy companies pay a high cost to pollute.

That said, the longevity of natural gas as an energy transition source depends on a few factors. The first one is emission limits. Extracting gas and transporting it in ways other than a pipeline is itself a process that generates emissions.

The second is related to technologies applicable to renewables. Wind farms, for example, are exposed to wind regimes that change not only between seasons but also between years. Managing this factor is one of the challenges, along with the development of long-lasting batteries.

Carbon markets

Nothing works without the right incentives. In order to induce businesses to reduce their emission levels, governments either adopt carbon pricing (the most common) or impose a carbon tax.

Pollution permits are traded either in a regulated environment or voluntarily. In the regulated market, "cap and trade" policy is adopted, meaning that companies have a limit to pollute (cap), while at the same time they can negotiate their permits (trade).

The voluntary market, on the other hand, is based on offsets. In this model, agents negotiate credits generated by clean projects. More polluting companies buy them in order to compensate for what they release in the atmosphere. Unlike the regulated market, most participate for reputational reasons.

Imbalances such as the supply shocks seen in 2021 show why subsidies and price controls are so tricky. That said, how do economies push forward the energy transition without angering the population?

Until recently, the answer was natural gas.

CHAPTER 20

UNAFFORDABLE HOUSING

Airing of protest images is something Chinese authorities avoid at all costs. However, with the struggles faced by companies such as Evergrande, it became difficult to hide an obvious finding: the high prices of real estate in China.

Over the past 15 years, prices jumped by more than 10% per year in the most important cities. In order to understand this impressive growth, one has to go back to 1994, when the Chinese government overhauled its tax system.

Local governments, having lost most of their revenue and unable to issue debt, had to count on the sale of land in order to meet the growth targets demanded by Beijing. Consequently, in the years preceding the 2008 crisis, many rural regions were transformed into urban areas that, once sold to developers, accounted for more than 70% of local public budgets.

Real estate assets

For cultural reasons, Chinese are fond of real estate assets. In a traditional portfolio, property holds a share close to 60% of the total. Hence, a large part of the population's debt is linked to real estate financing.

As leverage was limited by Chinese authorities, many builders focused on pre-sales, deals where interested parties pay upfront for properties that will only exist in the future. So, in the face of a major bankruptcy, the government had to act.

President Xi Jinping's "common prosperity" aims to address this issue. The secret is to get rid of such excesses without slowing the economy, which is already facing the chaotic implementation of other public policies amidst an energy crisis (as explained in the previous chapter).

Referendum

Berlin is another example of how inaccessible housing has become in large cities. On September 26th, a referendum, held together with the elections, had the purpose of deciding whether the city should expropriate approximately 240,000 properties held by major real estate companies.

Although non-binding (with no effect), the result (56.4% in favor) left many institutional investors such as REITs, insurance companies and pension funds alert.

Mismatch

As observed in other parts of the world, real estate values have skyrocketed in the last decade, meaning that wages no longer kept up with rents.

After the 2008 crisis, a group of financial institutions invested heavily in foreclosed homes. Over the years, what used to be a niche activity spun off into new businesses, becoming publicly traded real estate companies instead.

With their pockets full, they shopped around for the best places, guaranteeing a pipeline of projects for construction sites. As a result, average people were left out, even when counting with premium financing.

Public policies that impose some form of control hardly work. In a Spanish city that tried to limit lease prices, the market as a whole became smaller, with prices remaining at the same level.

Returning to Berlin, which has even tested a rental freeze for a period of 5 years, the number of properties available for lease was also smaller.

Macroprudential rules

Would macro-prudential measures be an option to fix it? Although they are aimed at the stability of the financial system, it is argued that they could also curb rising property prices by limiting debt levels.

Unlike monetary policy, which only makes financing more expensive, macroprudential rules have greater flexibility, whether to set financing according to the property's value ("loan-to-value"), whether to define financing in terms of income ("loan-to-income").

The downside is in its unwanted effects. Even if prices increase at a slower pace, credit becomes harder to obtain, as fewer participants are willing to lend. For now, institutional investors will continue playing a significant role, as real estate acts as a hedge against inflation (as explained in chapter 17).

Scenes of protest and revolt aside, construction sites suffer from the same supply restrictions as other sectors of the economy. With less places to live, housing will probably remain expensive in the foreseeable future.

CHAPTER 21

THIRD WAVE

More than just a distraction for brilliant minds, real time data has been used to find some rationality in the global chaos generated by a sequence of supply shocks (lack of supplies, lack of fuel and electricity and, more recently, lack of labor).

Looking at so many disconnected events, the big question is: given this scenario, how to assess inflation expectations? This leads to a second, more important question.

If these same expectations guide interest rates in countries that follow inflation targeting regimes, are central banks properly prepared to decide based on the information they receive before each monetary policy meeting?

Inflation

To measure inflation, you need an index. Although quite simple, this principle is far from perfect. First, because consumer preferences change over time, altering what needs to be measured and, second, because it has never been tested in a pandemic situation.

For no other reason, main central banks have adopted inflation rates slightly above target. Occasions in the past have made clear how inappropriate early interest rate hikes can be. When observing the latest oil shock, for example, many point to a decision taken in July 2008.

At that time, the European Central Bank (ECB) raised interest rates to fight an inflationary process due to an increase in oil prices, at a time when the continent was already in recession. In 2011, the same monetary policy mistake, throwing Europe into the abyss.

Expectations

Could a Federal Reserve (Fed) researcher cause a rethink?

This is the case of Jeremy Rudd, who turned the concept of inflation expectations upside down, defying the belief of inflation as a "self-fulfilling prophecy".

In other words, if employees and companies expect higher costs in the future, both will ask for higher wages and prices, respectively. Thus, the job of central banks is to "break" this expectation through higher interest rates.

Rudd, who has been studying the subject for at least 20 years, argues that this idea does not hold. If expectations are formed with the coming months as a reference, how could central banks decide for the following years?

The researcher goes further. Before the pandemic, productivity gains resulting from globalization kept costs and wages low. As a result, persistently low global inflation led to subdued expectations.

His work concludes that so much attention to expectations can lead to big mistakes. Initially, because it's actual prices that matter and, as long as there are no big changes, society at large ignores what central banks do.

Number crunching

New situations, such as a pandemic, require new responses. That said, wouldn't it be the case of reviewing current models, taking into account how the economy has changed?

To answer this question, nothing better than to collect and interpret real time data, as official information such as GDP growth and unemployment levels are released late, and still subject to revisions.

The world is embracing the "third wave" of economics. The

first began in the 18th century with Adam Smith and his theoretical work. The second, in turn, came with Keynesianism and its respective reversal, as defended by Milton Friedman.

Leading central banks are already exploiting it. Computers crunching mobility data and financial transactions are part of a bigger project, Central Bank Digital Currencies (CBDCs), as explained in chapter 10, which theoretically could show everything about how the economy works.

The result of this change is that, instead of interest rate decisions that take full effect after a year and a half, immediate and targeted actions, such as granting credit to groups that meet certain requirements. This would replace much of the bureaucratic and often ineffective government programs.

A new way of thinking macroeconomics, with very practical uses, is substituting the old fashioned, theoretical aspect of the field.

CHAPTER 22

GLOBAL VENTURE

Venture Capital (VC), as explained in chapter 16, is the type of business that fosters innovation.

Looking back, there is a lot to celebrate: 70% of the world's largest companies grew through VC funds, which have financed everything from electric vehicles to vaccines.

Nascent in the 60s, they invest in companies whose main product is an idea. As fanciful as this may be, this niche already accounts for approximately US$ 18 trillion in market capitalization. This number tends to increase, as new ventures go public, pushed mainly by institutional investors trapped between low interest rates and overvalued assets.

As the pandemic digitalized many sectors, roughly half of VC transactions already take place outside the US. That said, the next big opportunity is no longer in Silicon Valley. As global venture takes over the world, new investors are pilling in.

This move is led by the private equity industry, bringing in a bigger pool of alternatives such as clean energy technologies and biotech.

Losses

As mentioned before, VC is an area where, for every 10 bets, 1 pays off exceptionally well, making up for all the rest. For no other reason, it attracts all kinds of people, meaning money does not necessarily go to companies that will become sector winners.

Broadly speaking, of 100 startups that went public in 2021, more than half made no profit. Even before the IPO, many lose their appeal, as with each new investment round, everyone's participation is diluted, reducing gains even for those that joined first.

Despite this, many funds still prefer disruptive technologies than overly expensive markets ready for a reversal. After all, startups do not raise funds through debt (intangibles such as intellectual property are hardly accepted as collateral), which limits the damage once they shut their doors.

Throughout the years, venture capital has reinvented itself, especially after technology groups stopped purchasing new startups, fearful of a government agenda of greater control and higher taxation.

Many act as traditional asset managers, forming a portfolio of startups. Others fall into the angel investor category. This is the case of the founder who sells his own company and sets up a fund with the proceeds.

As many startups end up going public, it is common for VC houses to recycle the money. This means that, instead of returning funds to investors after a period of 10 years, they direct their IPO shares to a new fund category, snapping up any further appreciation.

Trends

With the arrival of the fourth wave of the pandemic (omicron), it is very likely that new ideas will form a pipeline of promising deals. Today, innovation is no longer exclusive to Silicon Valley, where founders and VC funds used to mingle.

New members have joined the group, due to two factors:

low interest rates and the obvious finding that any large publicly traded company can cease to exist if the next disruptive idea takes hold.

VC funds, previously more segmented, had to adapt and evolve. It's no longer about launching the next Uber or Airbnb.

The future of innovation involves choosing the company with the best chances of developing treatments for severe diseases or the technology that will raise living standards in the poorest regions of the planet. Whether idealism goes hand-in-hand with profits remains an open question.

Globally speaking, startup IPOs in 2021 added nearly US$ 500 billion. For the next big business to emerge, all it takes is just one more successful idea.

CHAPTER 23

THE FUTURE

What to expect of 2022? In order to answer this question, one must ponder on the many variables shaping the world economy.

Beginning with inflation. After a series of supply shocks, will it maintain its temporary nature, making central banks rather wait than act? Many argue that raising rates will not increase oil output or make people go back to work. Nonetheless, the beginning of 2022 will be inflationary.

That imposes new challenges. If new lockdowns become necessary, it will be impossible to use large scale stimulus programs again. Central bankers then will be forced to step on the brakes to cool off prices, especially if the energy transition proves trickier than expected.

Whatever the decision, most of the action will take place in another sphere of finance. Much cheaper and with less regulatory constrains than the traditional financial system, decentralized finance (DeFi) will take the lead in innovation.

Although it does not have much use in the real economy, that could change as parts of it are implemented in routine activities, as the adoption of Bitcoin by El Salvador shows. Another possibility would come from registering ordinary assets such as bonds and stocks on the blockchain.

Prospects could not be more promising. The pandemic digitized many parts of economic activity. As digital content gains heft, a new real economy could emerge through the DeFi structure and its self-executing contracts.

Society, although still struggling with the "new normal", will definitely maintain some of the changes imposed by the pandemic. That said, it is naïve to think that macro-economic policy will not have to tackle unforeseen issues, changing the way investments are made and assets are priced.

This by itself is already an exciting topic for next year's book.

Happy 2022!

All rights reserved.

ABOUT THE AUTHOR

Nohad T. Harati

NOHAD T. HARATI has a degree in business administration in addition to both an MBA in finances and an LLM in financial market law from a prestigious Brazilian educational institution (Insper).

She started her career at a local commodities broker, becoming a private banking investment analyst for a Swiss financial institution a few years later.

She also participated as an alternate board member at Companhia Energética de Minas Gerais (CEMIG), a Brazilian energy distribution company.

Currently, she manages a proprietary portfolio, runs a family office and is a regular columnist for the Brazilian investment startup Mais Retorno (https://maisretorno.com/portal/autor/nohadharati) in addition to publishing articles in her own personal pages:
LinkedIn: https://www.linkedin.com/in/nohadharati/
Quora (English): https://www.quora.com/profile/Nohad-Harati
Quora (Portuguese): https://pt.quora.com/profile/Nohad-Harati